I0500211

PAGE ONE MAGIC

Discover How To Get Multiple Page One Search Engine Rankings In A Couple Of Days For Your Local Website Or Your Local Business So That You Can: Generate More Leads, Dominate Your Local Market, And Make More Money For Your Business.

By
Al Hemmings

TABLE OF CONTENTS

CHAPTER 1

WHY YOU SHOULD READ THIS ENTIRE BOOK TODAY

IT WILL SHOW YOU HOW TO GET MORE TRAFFIC FASTER, AND HELP YOU TO MAKE MORE MONEY FOR YOUR BUSINESS

WHO IS THE PAGE ONE MAGIC SYSTEM FOR?

- Anyone who wants to test local business search terms to see what will rank on page one quickly.

- Anyone who wants local page one rankings for their local business search terms.

- Anyone who wants more local leads and enquiries for their business than their competitors.

- Anyone who doesn't want to wait months and years to get traffic from Google.

- Anyone who already has an existing local business website.

- Anyone who is just starting a new local business website.

- Anyone who has got a brand new website that offers local services and products.

- Anyone who is serious about local marketing and making a success of their online business.

- Anyone who wants to turn page one rankings into money.

- And anyone who isn't already on the first page of Google.

SO:

If you've been struggling to get traffic to your website.

If you want to be on page one of Google.

If you want results like those shown in the demo video.

If you want to dominate and outrank your competitors at will.

If you want to get more phone calls than your competition.

If you are serious about your online marketing.

If you want to make a success of your online business and you need help, then this is definitely for you.

In this book I will give you all of reasons why you should get the products in the system and use them in your own business.

Further on in this book there is a link to a demo video which will show you how you can become number one in your niche and how to crush your local competitors. If you feel that it is something that will help you, all you need to do is to sign up and you will get my **FREE BONUS GIFT.** The bonus gift will give you more information on where to get the products that will get you more customers and make more money for your business.

CHAPTER 2

WOULDN'T IT BE NICE

Have you ever wished that you could rank on Google (with ease) for search terms that people are using to find your local business or products?

Have you ever wondered what search terms will get onto page one before you lift a finger to set up your new local business?

Do you currently have a local business website and would like to get lots of page one rankings for that site?

Are you frustrated or fed up of not getting more leads, enquiries and sales each month?

Are you tired of playing second fiddle to your local business competitors?

Are you thinking about starting your own local business and worried that it could fail because you may not get enough customers to your website?

Are you fed up of using expensive website SEO companies and their old hat solutions that take forever to work?

If you have said yes to any of the above, then I would recommend that you invest in the software's that are in this system because they will help you to fix all of those problems.

One of the major problems that most local business owners have is that they don't know how (or where) to get more local traffic to their websites and products. I have noticed that there are a lot of Internet marketers out there who are teaching people complicated methods that will either waste a lot of your time; cost you a lot of money, or both.

How many of us have got unlimited amounts of money to spend on things that don't really work?

Paid advertising (or paid traffic) is said to be the fastest way to get traffic, but if you start off with paid advertising there tends to be a period in the beginning where you will probably lose money before you find out what actually works. Even if you do know what you're doing, this test phase may still cost you lots more money before you start breaking even. For the majority of newbies, even a small amount of money used to buy paid ads can quickly turn into a large money pit.

What sane person wants to be paying Google for traffic that doesn't buy anything from them?

I don't know about you, but I don't like anything that's going to help my online business to fail.

Most of you will have never done Keyword Research before, or used the Google Keyword Planner tool. If you haven't done either of these things, you won't be aware of how important keyword research is to the success of an Internet-based business.

If you want to appreciate and understand the importance of keyword research and would like to effectively leverage it in your business then you will definitely benefit from searching YouTube and watching some of the KEYWORD RESEARCH videos.

There are lots of videos on YouTube that show you how to use the Google Keyword Planner Tool and after you have watched some of these videos, the Page One Magic System will become clearer and make a lot more sense.

You will need to setup a GMAIL email account to gain access to the Keyword Planner tool; this only takes about 5 minutes.

Wouldn't it be fantastic if you could simply and easily, test and rank for the search terms that people will use to find your local business? Wouldn't it be nice if you could use a method that costs very little money? Of course it would.

I know for a fact that all local businesses want to get more visitors to their website, they also want to generate more local leads, get lots of FREE targeted traffic, and they would like to rank their business on page one of Google's search results.

In this book, I will talk about a specific method that you can use to get your local business on page one of Google. The system that I am talking about and recommending; is fantastic for local businesses who want to get more traffic and leads to their website. The end result is that you will make more money.

This not a system that will go out of date because it is based on how Google ranks web properties on page one.

Sometimes you have to think outside of the box and apply methods, strategies and techniques that will get you the biggest leverage for your efforts, i.e. time and money. You also want them to give you a big advantage over your competitors.

I wrote this short book to tell you about what I am using to get local traffic for fun, so I know that it does work. I am one of those people who will not recommend anything to anyone else unless I've tried it for myself.

In the following pages, I'm going to show you how I can get multiple page one rankings in Google for any local business within a few hours, using a system that I call PAGE ONE MAGIC.

WHAT IS PAGE ONE MAGIC?

Page One Magic is not the name of any products, it's what I have called this fantastic (and very fast) system which ranks multiple web properties on page one of Google, and gets more local visitors to your website.

Page One Magic can save you weeks and months of wasted time, by letting you know which of the search terms will hit page one of Google. You can now find out this information within a day.

If you're thinking about setting up a local business website, it will stop you wasting time and effort, and spending weeks and months finding out that the search terms (keywords) that you chose, did not (or will not) make the first page of Google. In most cases, if you're not on the first page of a search engine like Google, you'll probably struggle to make any money.

The software that is used shows you with 100% proof all of the search terms that will be on page one.

Once everything is setup, all you do is add a link and a phone number that points back to your local website, or your product page.

Even if you have got the best website and products on the planet, if you don't get enough traffic to your site you will not make any money. If no one can find your site, or if nobody is visiting your site, you're not going to get many online sales. It is really that simple.

If you're just getting started in online marketing and you want to build a successful local online business, there are now some fantastic products available that will help you to succeed faster than ever.

One of the main things that people who are new to online marketing tend to forget about is the fact that they need to get traffic to their website. If you're thinking of using a website to generate sales, then you will need to learn how to generate traffic and get people to your site.

Traffic is the one thing that everyone needs to be successful online, but nobody seems to be telling you how really important it is, or how to get it. Once you've conquered traffic generation, you will always make money online.

BUYER TRAFFIC is what everyone should go after, and the lack of this type of traffic is one of the main reasons why most people's online businesses fail.

Most people have this **'Field of Dreams'** idea where they think that '**If you build it they will come'**. Unfortunately, in the majority of cases it just doesn't work that way on the Internet.

You will have to do some work to get traffic to your website, products, articles, etc.

Just like a lot of newbies who set up websites and try to make money online, I also struggled in the beginning, but as soon as I started using the page one magic system everything changed for me because the system immediately helped me to overcome my traffic getting problems.

I have created a demo video that shows you the type of results you can achieve by using the system.

I could really hype up the video but that's just not my style. Just watch the video and you will see the PROOF for yourself.

Go to: **www.pageonemagic.co.uk**

In the video you will discover how to:

- Find and get multiple page one Google rankings at will in hours for your local online website/business.

- Generate more leads and enquiries.

- Dominate and crush your local competition and make more money for your business.

It's like having 10, 20, 30, 40 or even 50+ lead generating page one resources that will get you more enquiries. The more phone calls you get, the more money you should make for your business. As you will see from the results in the video, it isn't really that difficult to do.

After you watch the demo video, just imagine that they are your resources, and you are ranking for lots of search terms that people are using to find your business on Google.

Just imagine if you were able to use the right search terms to dominate practically any local niche market at will and it didn't really matter how competitive that niche was!

If you have got a local website or business, it's an amazing system that allows you to rank for multiple search terms.

It means that you could double or even triple the number of visitors to your website and make a lot more money.

If you're not on the first page of Google for your local search terms, and you're relying solely on a website to:

- Get traffic

- Get leads and enquiries

- Generate sales, etc.

Unless you've been established online for a very long time and you're already getting enough traffic, or you have got a good offline business, you're probably going to struggle to survive online because you need to be getting lots of good quality traffic and leads. I know this to be a fact because in the beginning I really struggled to get any online sales.

From A to Z – whatever your type of business, whether you're an Accountant or a Zen Master, the page one magic system will probably help you.

The software allows you to test for search terms that will end up ranking on page one of Google; you will get the results within minutes after the test has been completed.

The thing that takes the longest is the video creation for those search terms. You have to create and upload videos and add some information. You don't need to panic or worry about video creation because there are some fantastic free and paid video creation software out there that are very easy to use. The software will make this process (and your life) so easy. Single and multiple videos are now very easy to create.

You can outsource video creation if you don't want to do it yourself, but it will be a lot more expensive. I suggest using either the free or paid software and do it yourself because it doesn't take that long, especially if you buy the paid software and use that to create multiple videos. The paid software will create up to 100 different videos for you, in one go.

This is the fastest page one ranking and traffic getting solution that I know of and it will get you more leads and enquiries quickly so that you can start crushing your competitors. I can tell you from my own experience that it doesn't get much easier than this.

It's time to stop following the herd and stop doing what everyone else is doing. Start doing traffic generation the right way and start using tools that actually work.

Let's say that you've got a business (it could be anything), you could be offering products and/or services locally or on a larger scale. Imagine that someone goes online and starts looking for information on something that you sell. Do you think that you might get a few more customers, clients, and sales, if your information was showing up on the first pages of the Google search results?

Of course you would.

If you use this system, you will be able to target those people who are searching for your products and services in your local market.

If you're new to online marketing you can use this system to test your market before you make any major investment in your new business. One of the great things about the system, is it allows you to test your markct first. It is much better to spend a couple hundred dollars and test your market than to spend tens of thousands setting up a business that may fail within the first 12 months.

For anyone who is just starting out, the easiest way to avoid a business failure is to test your local search terms for page one rankings, monthly traffic, and phone calls, before you commit to spending large amounts of money on advertising.

By using the methods, advice, and strategies mentioned in this book (and in my free bonus gifts), you will quickly see how many monthly searches each keyword gets and which keywords will end up on page one of Google. By finding out and using this information first, you will immediately know what keywords will drive more traffic to your website, (or web property), and what keywords you should use to get that traffic.

Setting up a new online business in a competitive market can take a long time and become a very expensive process, and if you focus on the wrong search terms (keywords), you will probably find out that your site will not get the results you want.

If an economic downturn ever happens, it could mean that your business competitors are more likely to go out of business than you are. The biggest difference between you and them is that you will have multiple rankings at the top of the search results, which means you will get a lot more traffic than they will.

It is a known fact that when people search online, they tend to only use the sites on the first page of the search results, and they mostly click on the top 3 organic websites (i.e. websites not paying for advertising). The top 3 organic positions could also include videos.

If you've got a local website, generally speaking it will be easier to rank for longer local search terms than for a main search term; for example, it would be much easier to rank for the search term **credit cards comparison**, than for the search term **credit cards**.

Search terms are compiled by using the following three things:

BUSINESS TYPE + AREA OF CITY + CONNECTING WORD

BUSINESS TYPE: dentist

AREA OF CITY: Florida

CONNECTING WORD: best

EXAMPLES OF COMPLETED SEARCH TERMS:

dentist Florida

Florida dentist

best dentist Florida

best Florida dentist

I have created 2 sample lists of search terms that I use in my business and you will get access to them when you sign up for my free bonus gifts. There are more than 150 search term examples and they are a good starting place to test for page one rankings for your own business, you just need to adjust the terms for your own business type.

The software that is used in the system allows you to upload and test 100 different search terms at a time, you can choose the option to also show the search terms that end up on page two aswell. Unless you have some knowledge about how to get backlinks, you should only use the search terms that end up on page one.

On the 7th April 2017 I came across a new web browser add-on tool that shows you the monthly search volume for each local or global keyword, the cost per click (CPC) information, and the competition data.

This is very helpful if you want to know roughly how many local (or global) searches your keyword gets each month. Once installed, the information is shown on each Google search results page, so it's right there in front of you. This is a very helpful tool for using as part of your traffic market research.

PAID ADVERTISING:

Paid online advertising charges you every time someone clicks on your ad, if you use proper Google safe optimisation and the page one magic system, the same traffic that Google wants you to pay good money for, now becomes 100% FREE to you.

If you use the system properly, you won't need to think about paying Google any money for ads to get page one traffic. One of the best things about the system is that you don't have to worry anymore about not having a website on page one of Google. The system will drive traffic to your site no matter what page of the search engines your website is on.

All of these page one rankings will allow you to CRUSH your local business competitors because you will get lots more extra visitors (FREE TRAFFIC) to your website. The end result of using the system is that you'll make more money.

THIS IS A POWERUL SYSTEM FOR YOUR BUSINESS

This is not a system that tries to fool Google either, because nowadays you'll quickly get found out and end up with a Google slap or penalty. If you want it to work long term, you need to play by Google's rules because, if you don't, there will only be one winner, and it won't be you.

Search engine rankings and search results have always been about giving the top positions for a given keyword or search phrase to the most relevant and popular site, video, website content, or information, etc.

The page one magic system uses a method whereby the software will query Google and get it to tell you which of your search terms will rank on page one. You then link those page one rankings to your website, or web properties. SIMPLE!!

YOU NEED TO GET TARGETED TRAFFIC

If you have got a local website or a local online business you will be well aware of how important it is to get visitors to your site.

You need to target those people who are actually looking for what you are offering, because that is how you will make your money. It's no good if these people are going to page one and you're not there.

The main problem with websites is this: only ten of them are allowed on page one of Google. So unless you've got a bricks and mortar business as a backup, you're probably going to struggle to get customers and make sales from your website if you're not on page one of the search results. If you're relying solely on your website and that website is not on page one, you're going to have serious problems getting traffic.

Unless you use this system, being on the second page of Google (or worse) is no good if you want to make a success of your local online business.

CHAPTER 3

MY FAILURES TURNED INTO SUCCESS

Over the last two years of running my own online businesses, what I've learned is that before I do anything I always ask myself these five questions, and they are:

IS THERE MONEY IN THAT MARKET?

WHERE IS MY TRAFFIC COMING FROM?

WHERE ARE MY BUYERS COMING FROM?

HOW EASY IS IT TO GET TRAFFIC?

WHAT STRATEGIES DO I HAVE IN PLACE TO GET THE TRAFFIC?

If you don't know the answer to these questions, you are more likely to fail online faster than you realise.

I do understand the realities and the problems of not getting any traffic, because early in my online career I made mistakes – a lot of mistakes.

I was in too many markets and I lost focus on the real goal of my business.

I wanted to be known as the authority in my niche(s).

I wanted to build a long lasting business via my websites.

I wanted to make a lot of money.

In my first 18 months, I learnt so much about websites that I decided to do everything myself. I became really good at setting up websites but I wasn't getting any visitors (traffic) to my sites.

When I first started online, I came across many website training courses and some of them claimed that they could get your local website onto the first page of Google within three months. I tried all of their methods but my local websites still didn't get onto page one of Google within that timescale. One of the sites did go up the rankings but ended up on page ten of the Google searches. Just to let you know, being on page ten didn't make me any money

I was doing what all the so-called gurus were telling me to do and I was still getting NO TRAFFIC.

I spent hundreds of hours testing and learning, I started buying more and more training courses, but in the end I just wasted lots of money. I was trying black hat and white hat loopholes and techniques but none of these things really worked. After a while I started suffering from information overload and burnout because I was trying to do too many things. I was struggling so much that I was ready to call it a day and give up.

During my first 18 months online, I made the sum total of $120 from my websites so, as you can see, I do know what it's like to not make any money online. What kept me going was the knowledge that I had made some money so I knew that something was working. By now I realised that all I needed to do was to find a system that worked well and that I could upscale.

I realised that good quality traffic is the lifeblood of all online businesses and that my success online would depend on getting this type of traffic to my website, products, offers, etc. I knew that if I didn't start getting visitors quickly, my online business was going to fail and I would give up.

As you can see, I was hardly making any money, and as we all know, fresh air doesn't pay the bills.

After doing some more investigation, I found out that I would need a lot more specialised software tools and a lot more money. Most people who want to get their website onto the first page of Google end up paying an SEO (Search Engine Optimisation) company a small fortune to get their sites ranked on page one. This was not a particular route that I wanted to go down.

In October 2016 I came across something that worked like magic and that's why I wrote this book to tell you about it. It's a system that works with Google, YouTube, and the other search engines and it doesn't use methods and tactics that will get you banned, blocked, or shut down.

With this system you are guaranteed page one rankings in minutes, it works so well that if you do it right; it is possible to eventually completely take over your local niche market.

Traditional search engine ranking methods are hard, boring, and expensive. Those methods can be very slow and time consuming, and if you don't know what you're doing it will never work for you.

If you're anything like me, you want something that is easy to learn, it's fast and effective, and it just works.

This system is exactly that, it does what it says on the tin. You input your search terms (keywords) and you let the software find you those golden nuggets that will rank on page one of Google and bring traffic to your website, or web property.

Most people don't want to spend lots of money on SEO or wait months or even years to see if their sites will start getting traffic. This brings you back to one of the biggest problems for you if you're a website owner;

there are only ten positions available for websites on page one of Google.

I wasted a lot of time, money and energy, and got nowhere, but I still knew that that the first page of Google was the only place to be. I was really struggling to get anywhere near those top ten website positions, so I started wondering what other alternatives were out there?

Well, there is Google Adwords where you can pay Google for an advert, but depending on what niche or market your business is in; you will found that those ads can cost a lot of money. I don't know if you know this but you will still pay Google money if someone clicks on your ad, they go to your website, and they buy nothing.

Another thing to think about is this, what if Google only allows five ads on the first page and your ad is number six? It means that you'll be spending money hoping that people will also search page two of Google, because that is the page your ad will be on.

Now ask yourself this, how many times can you honestly say that you go and search page two of Google for something that you're looking for? The truth is, not many of us do it. Nine times out of ten what we want and what we're looking for is usually on page one.

Google's algorithms say that everything that is on page one for a search term is the best, this includes the ads at the top and bottom of a search page results. If you don't see any ads on a page of a search result, this tends to mean that there is not a lot of money to be made from advertising there, but there are exceptions to this.

This isn't a problem for you because you won't be paying for any advertising; it really doesn't matter to you whether or not there are any paid ads on the search page results, all you're after is the traffic from the page one search terms.

If you look at all the odds, they certainly seem to be stacked against you if you're not on page one. I've read somewhere that page one of Google gets about 95% of the traffic for searches. That's quite a frightening statistic if you're trying to run a business through a website and you're not on page one, and you're not using this system.

Most people are fortunate because they have a bricks and mortar business premises, a shop or a store, and they make some money that way.

The thing is though, if you're in competition against other people in your local area who have got a similar type of business, then you need an immediate edge and an advantage over them. This is what this system gives you.

CHAPTER 4

HOW DID I MANAGE TO FIND A SOLUTION?

In October 2016 I came across a system that allowed me to query Google for local search terms that people use to find local online websites and use the ones that are on page one to drive more traffic to those sites.

Can you believe it? Instead of waiting months and years to know what search terms people will find your local business with, you can find out within a day.

I personally have bought the products used in this system and I can honestly say that, if you have a local business, if you have a website that isn't on page one of Google, or if you're just setting up a new local website, this is probably going to be the best money you'll ever spend to get people to your website and to make more money.

Over the last couple of years I've spent a lot of money on many products that claim a lot of things, but this is the first system that I have found that can actually help someone to start getting more local traffic and phone calls within 2–3 weeks from a standing start.

By using the system, you will never have to worry again about not getting any traffic to your local website. It doesn't matter now if your website is on page two of Google or page five hundred, you will get traffic and you will start dominating your niche and crushing your local competitors.

Below are some other methods you can use to generate traffic to your website or products.

You can get traffic from:

YOUR OWN YOUTUBE VIDEOS AND YOUTUBE PAID ADS

PAYING FOR GOOGLE ADS (Google Adwords)

FACEBOOK MARKETING AND FACEBOOK COMMENTING

SOCIAL MEDIA

TWITTER

COMMENTING ON FORUMS

BUYING SOLO ADS

HIGH TRAFFIC WEBSITES (that accept banner ads, etc.)

The above list isn't exhaustive but it is a start, some of them are very time consuming for getting traffic, and at the end of the day if you're in a local market, some of them may not be very useful for getting local traffic.

There are many traffic-getting methods, but the one that will cost you the least amount of money in the long run is page one magic. I have been using this collection of software myself to test and find search terms that I can rank for on the first page of Google, and I can tell you that this system will work for practically any local business.

CHAPTER 5

PROOF OF PAGE ONE RANKINGS

If you want to see proof of the page one rankings you can achieve, please go to the website below and watch the video.

www.pageonemagic.co.uk

These types of results were unheard of until NOW!!...

We're talking about getting first page rankings for search terms that people are using every day to find your type of business on Google. In some cases (as you will see) you may even get multiple rankings on the first page.

We are talking about getting traffic/visitors to your local website, products, or offers, very quickly.

I know of people who have spent £5,000 (approximately $6,000) or more trying to get similar results and their solution providers haven't even come close to what this system does.

If you don't use this system, how else are you ever going to achieve results like those in the video?

Yes, you could try to do this yourself but the problems that you will face are these:

1. You won't know if any of the videos you upload will rank in Google – By using the page one magic system you will know straight away.

2. You don't know the secret techniques to use to get those rankings on page one – **I do**.

Chapter 6

STOP SEARCHING FOR GOLD – START OWNING THE GOLDMINE

If you're not serious about your online business then this isn't for you, I say this because there is more than enough proof and evidence in the demo video that shows the type of results you can get.

For the two computer repair searches that I did, I input 100 search terms for each local area and I got 52 and 56 page one rankings respectively from the 200 searches. Many of these search terms are buyer intent searches.

The results in the demo video were the only search terms that Google would allow me to rank for on page one. You could get more, you could get less; it all depends on:

Google's algorithms?

How many videos Google allows on page one?

What the competition is?

How expensive the search terms are?

Etc.

When you buy advertising from Google, it has a value for each of the search terms. For example, a plastic surgeon search term will cost a lot more money in Google's paid ads than a computer repair search term.

The special software allows you to get your test search results back within minutes after completion, but I tend to leave the results alone for a couple of days to let things settle before I go back and check them.

WHAT ARE THE SOFTWARE AND TOOLS THAT ARE NEEDED?

1. A special software for testing which of your local search terms will rank on page one. It will also upload your videos.

2. A software for creating multiple videos.

3. An article creator that creates multiple articles from a single article, also known as an article spinner. Each video needs its own article for the description content box – there is paid software that will do this, or you can use a free online article spinner.

4. A YouTube channel – there is a special type of YouTube channel that is used for uploading the final videos; this channel and the other associated

web properties will help the videos to stick on page one. There is a small cost involved to setup the channel.

5. *Professional stock image photos for your videos – there are some good places where you can go get high quality images at good prices to use on your videos for your business.

6. *Someone to do voiceovers – if you want to add speech to your videos, this is applicable if you don't think you have a nice sounding voice.

7. Royalty Free Music – Is for if you don't want to use a voice in your videos – FREE

*If you decide that the page one magic system is something that you want for your business, I will show you where you can get *5 and *6 above done very cheaply. All will be revealed in my free bonus gifts.

CHAPTER 7

FAQ's

Q. What is PAGE ONE MAGIC and who is it for?

A. PAGE ONE MAGIC is a method of seeing if search terms that you put into Google will rank on the first page. It is a fantastic method of getting traffic and leads quickly. What we have found is that most websites and website SEO (Search Engine Optimisation) take too long to rank, i.e. months and years (if ever).

We no longer rely solely on our website to get us our traffic from Google because as I've pointed out, you can have a website on the Internet and not get any traffic at all. That's why we use the system to send traffic to our website. The beauty of this system is that it doesn't matter where your website is on Google, you will get traffic to it.

If you have got a local website, the most important (and only) place to be on Google is on the first page, this is because very few people ever go searching pages 2, 3, 4, etc. for what they want. As you've seen, you can use the system to get multiple page one rankings quickly and easily even if your website is not on page one.

These rankings will bring you that all important traffic and phone calls. If you're getting more phone calls, this usually means that you'll make more money. The system is the fastest and most successful way of achieving these very important things.

The system is for anyone who has a local business and who wants to be on the first page for search terms in their local area and surrounding areas. The first page of Google is where the money is and this is where it is now possible to have multiple listings.

This method could be the difference between having a successful online business, or failure.

Q. What makes it better than other "ranking" software out there?

A. First off all, it actually works, the team spent almost a year PERFECTING this powerful ranking software, and they've got examples of many people getting real results fast!

Q. How long does it take to rank these search terms?

A. It is possible to start seeing some of your page one test rankings within a few minutes after the test run has been completed, but what we suggest you do is to wait for a day or two to see what position they end up at. Google may bounce them up and down on the page for a day or so, but after that they eventually settle into a position on a page.

Q. How many of my search terms (keywords) can you rank for?

A. The software allows you to upload 100 search terms at a time. You won't know how many will rank until you do the test run. Google ultimately makes the final decision as to whether or not a search term/video will rank on page one, and how many?

Sometimes none will rank on page one, sometimes a single video will rank, other times you may get three videos or more ranking on page one so, as you can see, you don't have any say in the matter. That's why I said that you won't know the final positions until after you do a test run.

Q. How many will be in the number 1 position?

A. There are NO guarantees that any video will be in the number one position, this is particularly true if you try to rank for global search terms. Only Google knows what will happen but as you will see in the demo video, you should get a decent amount of number one positions for your local search terms.

Q. How long will the videos stay on page one?

A. How long is a piece of string? What you need to remember is that there are other companies out there that may be using their own strategies to rank websites and/or videos; this means that you may probably have some competition to stay on the first page. If your videos ever drop off the first page, there are people and places that you can go to get a video back to where it was.

As a general rule, if you use the special YouTube channel and web 2.0 package, you are less likely to lose your number one positions.

Q. What do I get in the SPECIAL YouTube package?

A. You get a YouTube video channel that is specially set up to help solidify and keep your page one rankings. Alongside the YouTube channel, you will also get some other social media sites like Facebook, Twitter, Google +, and other web 2.0 accounts, etc. These will all help to keep your videos in their positions on their respective pages.

Q. Will it work for all the local areas in my city?

A. Yes, this is a way to take over and dominate your city and its local surrounding areas.

When you do a search for something in your local area, for example: **plumber Boston**, you may notice that some people are paying for Google ads; these are usually at the top or the bottom of the page. If you want to know how much they are paying for those ads, phone them and speak to them nicely and find out how much they are paying for their advertising. This will give you an idea of how expensive the advertising is in comparison to this method.

What I have noticed and realised is this; whoever is on page one for a paid Google ad, the page one magic system always has a lot more page one rankings than that paid ad.

When I checked my 52 page one rankings for the computer repair searches, I noticed that a single ad (that was also on page one) was NOT on all of my 52 page one rankings. The ad may have shown up five or six times on page one, but not 52 times.

This is the massive advantage that you have over someone who is paying for Google ads. Based on a lot of feedback from people who use the software it seems like your search terms will give you (on average) ten times more exposure on page one than a single Google ad, it's amazing.

The other advantage that you have over the Google paid ads is this; every time that someone clicks on one of those ads, the advertiser (website owner) has to pay Google a fee; this payment method is known as PPC or Pay Per Click. This means that, if you're an advertiser and have created that ad, if someone clicks on your ad and they go to your site you have to pay Google money whether your visitor buys something from you or not.

Just supposing that you were paying £10 (approximately $13) per click to get traffic too your site, to my mind that's a lot of money that will be wasted on Google ads if you don't get any sales. I don't know about you, but I think that there are better ways of spending my money.

With the page one magic system, once your videos are on page one, you don't have that stupid PPC cost because no matter how many times someone goes to your website from your page one videos, you don't pay anybody for the privilege of that visit. Don't you think that this makes a lot more financial sense?

If you're curious and want to know how much someone is paying Google for that privilege, click on the ad, go to their website, contact them and ask them. Just say to them that you are thinking about buying Google Ads and ask how much it is costing them each month to be on page one for that ad.

Q. Does this system work for global search terms?

A. Yes it does, but it is a lot harder to rank for global search terms because there is a lot more competition worldwide. I've done many global searches and on some occasions I haven't had a single page one ranking from those searches, whereas when you do local searches you should get lots of page one rankings every time, because believe it or not there is less competition.

As you saw in the demo video I got as many as 56 page one rankings for local search terms. That's the difference between global and local searches.

Q. Do you have a list of search terms I can use to get me started?

A. Yes. Once you sign up one of the free gifts will provide you with two sample lists of local search terms; this is what I use and adapt for different niche markets and it's what I used in the demo video.

All you need to do is to change the names to your own local town and change the niche market, then start killing it by going after the other local surrounding areas. You will soon start taking over.

Q. What is the Google Auto Suggest?

A. This was originally created by Google and it monitors all search queries used in their search engine. Google stores them in a database and ranks them via popularity. It is also known as the Google Auto complete.

When you search for a word or phrase in Google, it helps you out by providing the auto complete suggestions in a drop down list while you're typing in your search term. It offers you the most relevant terms based on volume of searches, and what other people have already entered into the search engine. These search results will be similar to (and related to) what you're searching for. It's an incredibly powerful tool for marketers to use to get additional search terms for getting page one rankings.

Studies show that about 71% of people who use Google for searching also use the auto suggest search terms. These are incredibly powerful terms to use and if you are ranking for these types of local suggested search terms there is a very high likelihood of getting a lot of traffic from them.

You can also use the related searches search terms at the bottom of a browser search page.

Q. What about searches on mobile devices?

A. More and more people are searching Google using mobile devices, I'm sure everyone knows this by now. Search terms on mobile devices will have a big impact on your business because on these devices, when the auto suggest drops down, it covers most of the main screen and the rest of the screen is taken up by the keyboard.

This practically forces people to use the auto suggested terms supplied by Google and if you're on page one for one or more of these search terms you will get a lot of traffic coming to your website, or web property from mobile devices.

Q. What about images for the videos and how many do I need?

A. Image sizes for videos should be a minimum of 1,280 pixels (Wide) x 720 pixels (High), this is the minimum size for HD videos and these sizes of images will fill the whole screen. We recommend that at least 10 images are used to create your videos.

Q. Can I supply my own images?

A. Yes, as mentioned in the previous question, they should all be a minimum of 1,280 pixels (Wide) x 720 pixels (High) for HD purposes.

Q. After I've tested my search terms, how long does it take to get everything set up?

A. Once you know what you are doing, I would say about two weeks. What takes the longest to do is the video creation and waiting for delivery of your special YouTube channel and the related sites.

N.B. You can set up your own normal YouTube channel and upload the completed videos to it, but your videos may not stick on page one for as long. You should never ever upload your final completed videos to a test channel. Your test channel (as the name suggests) is for testing for page one rankings only.

What we suggest you do is to set up two YouTube channels:

One is used purely for testing for page one rankings, and the other channel is your specially optimised YouTube channel and web 2.0 properties; this is the one you use for uploading the completed videos to.

Q. What's involved in the special YouTube Channel?

This will be additional work for you because you have to provide some information to the software support people, i.e. a logo, a bio (a short biographical profile of someone), a spun article, etc.

Article spinning is a search engine optimization (SEO) technique by which an article is spun into many versions of relevant content and posted on article directories, websites, web 2.0 sites, or other sources for backlinks. The extent to which Google and other search engines can detect or devalue spun content is not clear.

My free bonus gift document will explain more.

If you don't know how to set up a YouTube channel, there are people and places you can go to get it done quite quickly and cheaply, so don't worry about anything that you're thinking may be a hurdle or problem, or something you don't understand.

You will get help from my free bonus gifts, the software vendors and their support desk and other people who are in the relevant Facebook groups.

N.B. The special YouTube channel is created and setup by the vendor of the main software. This service can be bought by contacting them. For the long term preservation of your page one rankings, I do recommend that you do buy this service.

Q. How easy is it to create the videos?

A. There is special video software that will create up to 100 different videos. All you need to do is to add your images, add any music, voiceovers, and press the create button – THAT'S IT. You don't need to spend hours learning the software either; it's quite intuitive and easy to use.

Q. Will the software work on my Mac?

A. The main software is designed to run on Window 7 or greater. To run on Mac, you will need to run Windows 7+ via Parallels (Windows emulation software).

Q. Is there a refund period for the products?

A. Yes, there is normally a 30 day refund period for each product, so if you're not happy for any reason, you'll get a full refund.

Q. Is there a cost to get access to the FREE BONUS GIFTS?

A. There is a cost for the products themselves but there is no cost for my free bonus gifts.

Q. How much does it cost?

A. The costs will be revealed to people who are serious about their online business and who are interested in taking their local business to another level. Compared to the cost of paying for Google ads long term and the amount of business that you are losing by not getting page one traffic, it's very cheap.

Q. What do I have to do to get started?

A. All you need to do is to go to the **PAGE ONE MAGIC** website, watch the demo video and then enter your email address on the page. After that you will be directed to the free bonus gifts download page.

All the information about training and the cost of the products that make this system work is in one of the bonus gift documents.

Can you please leave a review on Amazon about this book and share your comments with others.

CHAPTER 8

FINAL WORDS

I cannot make the claim that this system will work for everyone. There are a lot of things in life whereby one person will do something and succeed and another person who tries something similar will be unsuccessful; that's life.

It all depends on how you go about it and what you do. What I will say though is this; the page one magic system does work for action takers. If you use the software and follow the instructions given, you will be amazed at the results that you will achieve.

The instructions in the training videos are quite short and will guide you through each process. I have added some additional information in my free gift that will help to make your life a lot easier; it has definitely helped me.

It may look like a lot of information at first but when you finally see and understand why you are doing the things you have to do, you will then understand why I said at the beginning of this book that there is a bit of work that you have to do to get those rewards. All I'm doing is underpinning your knowledge and helping you to understand some of the things that are involved in ranking, and getting traffic. Based on my own personal experience, I feel that you need to know about some of the other pieces in the jigsaw that will eventually make up the bigger picture.

It's a bit like learning to drive a car; it is up to you to practice so that you get better and become more skilled and knowledgeable. It is exactly the same with this system, it's not that difficult to do or setup but you do need more of an understanding of how all these things work together.

If you're still wondering if you should go ahead with it, all I can say is this; there are people out there who are making it work and are reaping the benefits and rewards. There are now many testimonials from people who are using the products and showing the successes that they are having. These are the same type of people who started out just like you and I (i.e. without any knowledge) and who are now having a lot more success with their local business websites.

You also have a 30 day money back guarantee, so you can try it and if you don't like it you can get your money back. You really don't have any excuses anymore; you now have a good opportunity to make practically any local businesses very successful (depending on the type of business).

Once you're competent in using the system, you could use it to promote to other local businesses that are in other niches. Just imagine the look on their faces when you go back to them in a couple of days and show them their page one rankings. In another 12 months you could have a successful business with many clients that you are making money from by having (or charging) a monthly fee for your support.

I've already mentioned that if you ever get stuck you should use the relevant support desks or FB fanpages, so there really are no excuses for not using the system to make a lot more money. If you keep waiting or procrastinating, how are you going to feel if your competitors start using the same system and possibly put you out of business?

One of the reasons that most people fail in life is because they're usually too scared to take a chance on a good opportunity when it is put in front of them. Most people seem to have a 9am to 5pm employee mentality and are unwilling to take the first steps to do things that could make them financially better off. I don't know what it as about some people, but they just seem to be addicted to STRUGGLING, it's quite sad when you see it.

You've got 30 days to try the system; this should be plenty of time to at least do some testing yourself to see how many page one rankings you will get for a business of your choice. Remember this, you don't even need to have a business setup at this moment in time, all you're doing is querying Google to see what you will get on page one if you did have a local business.

After you get your results, you can then go setup a local website with content knowing with 99.9% certainty that you will get traffic from your rankings. I have personally supplied you with a lot of additional help in my free bonus gifts document because the additional information will definitely help you. If it's not for you, then all you have to do is to ask the product vendors for a full refund.

You need to get in there before your competitors start hearing about it and because there are only so many positions that Google will allow on page one. If you don't get to those page one positions soon for your own business, your competitors will.

If you're having any problems or if you run into any difficulties, please contact the product vendors' support desks or their Facebook groups, and they will help you.

Some of you may think that the information in this book sounds very technical, well, it's not really.

Once you have watched the demo video, watched the product videos, and you have read the information in my bonus gifts, you will soon get an **AHA!!** moment because it will all make sense and you will see how easy it actually is. My bonus gifts are there to help you with some of the other things that the products don't tell you about.

Please remember that it will be much easier the second time you do it.

CONCLUSION

If You Want To Rank On Page One On Google, You Need To Get It Today.

How powerful is this competition crushing software? Well, even NEWBIES are getting multiple rankings on page 1 of Google within hours.

- You use the software to query Google to give you page one rankings at will.

- It's a fantastic solution that allows you to dominate the search engines.

- You can start dominating rankings with just a few minutes setup.

- You can rank on page one of Google for single and multiple competitive local search terms.

- You can target every nearby city and take over your local market.

- Just setup a few things then sit back and watch your search terms rank.

- You use local search term ranking software that is super simple to use.

- You will get more FREE traffic, enquiries and sales, a lot quicker and more often.

- No need to hand over stupid amounts of money to SEO (Search Engine Optimisation) companies anymore. Forget about waiting months and years to get traffic to your website.

- 30 day money back guarantee

YES... IT'S REALLY THAT SIMPLE.

IMPORTANT NOTICE:

We haven't recommended anything to you in this book that we aren't using ourselves, or that we wouldn't recommend to our own family and friends,

We stand behind everything that we have said because we know it works, but we always recommend that you do your own independent research and due diligence before purchasing anything.

*N.B. Not all of the search terms that people use to find your local business will rank on page one. Google has the final say as to whether or not a search term will rank on the first page (if at all), so it has nothing to do with you.

I would like to take this opportunity to thank all my friends, family and anyone who has helped me on my journey so far. I would also like to thank you for taking time to read this book and for any support that you may give to me.

For those of you who make the decision to jump on board and take hold of this fantastic opportunity, I wish you every success. Thanks for taking time to read this information. If you put it into practice, you too should also become more successful in your own business.

Please watch the demo video to see how you too can achieve similar results.

DEMO VIDEO LINK: **www.pageonemagic.co.uk**

NEED A MENTOR TO HELP YOU
GROW YOUR BUSINESS?

Most successful entrepreneurs start off by learning from someone who is respected and already very successful in their industry, they realise that they should invest in a tutor and mentor so that they themselves can become more successful, and I'm no different.

The idea for the PAGE ONE MAGIC system training was given to me by my mentor, Christopher Payne. He is a highly respected and trusted marketing expert. Chris is helping, guiding and supporting me with my own Internet Marketing business. Chris advises beginners and people who make 6 and 7 figure incomes each year.

If you are interested in working with Chris, here's a link to his site:
www.christopherjohnpayne.com

DID YOU ENJOY THIS BOOK?

I want to thank you for purchasing and reading this book and I really hope you got a lot out of it. Can I ask a quick favour please? If you enjoyed this book I would really appreciate it if you could leave me a positive review on Amazon. I love getting feedback from my customers and reviews on Amazon really do make a difference. I read all my reviews and would really appreciate your thoughts.

If you need any additional help or support I can be contacted at: **al@pageonemagic.co.uk** - Thanks so much.

Alvet Hemmings

DISCLAIMERS AND TERMS OF USE

The author and publisher of this book and all accompanying providers have used all of their best efforts and intentions in preparing this material. The author and publisher make no representation or warranties with respect to the accuracy, applicability, fitness or completeness of the contents of this e-Book. The information contained in this book is strictly for educational purposes. Therefore, if you wish to apply any of the ideas contained in this book, you are taking full responsibility for your actions.

The author and publisher disclaim any warranties (express or implied), merchantability, or fitness for any particular purpose. The author and publisher shall in no event be held liable to any party for any direct, indirect, punitive, special, incidental or other consequential damages arising directly or indirectly from any use of this material, which is provided "as is" and without warranties.

The author and publisher do not warrant the performance, effectiveness or applicability of any sites or products that are mentioned, listed, or linked to in this book. All links, videos and other materials are for information purposes only and are not warranted for content, accuracy or any other implied or explicit purpose.

At the end of the demo video, it says that we setup your channel for you, this is not the case. The setting up of the YouTube channel only applies for customers and clients who we personally work with. There is a special YouTube channel package available from one of the product vendors where they will setup your YouTube channel and other related web 2.0 accounts for you; these include Twitter, Wordpress, Facebook, etc.

The results that you see in the demo video are test rankings to show you what results are possible. The videos for those test results may have since been removed from the test channel as most clients do not want their page one rankings (for their niche or business) being shown to other people, or their competitors, this is understandable.

The author, the product vendors, the manufacturers and distributors assume no liability or responsibility for any personal financial loss to persons, property or business that may happen as a result of wrongful or irresponsible use of the products purchased.

Affiliate Disclaimer:

We have an affiliate or marketing relationship with the companies, products and services mentioned. If you go on to purchase any of the products that the author of this book has reviewed, the author will receive compensation from those companies. We test each product thoroughly and give high marks to only the very best. We are independently owned and the opinions expressed here are our own.

www.ingramcontent.com/pod-product-compliance
Lightning Source LLC
Chambersburg PA
CBHW060149200526
45165CB00023B/1428